Animals of the

Bottlenose Dolphin

By Edana Eckart

Children's Press®
A Division of Scholastic Inc.
New York / Toronto / London / Auckland / Sydney
Mexico City / New Delhi / Hong Kong
Danbury, Connecticut

Photo Credits: Cover copyright © Brandon Cole; pp. 5, 9 © Gerard Lacz/Animals Animals; pp. 7, 13 © Tom Walmsley/Nature Picture Library; p. 11 © Mark Stouffer/Animals Animals; pp. 15, 17 © Jeffrey L. Rotman/Corbis; p. 19 © Tom Brakefield/Corbis; p. 21 © John Stern/ Animals Animals
Contributing Editor: Jennifer Silate
Book Design: Mindy Liu

Library of Congress Cataloging-in-Publication Data

Eckart, Edana.
  Bottlenose dolphin / by Edana Eckart.
  v. cm.—(Animals of the world)
  Contents: Bottlenose dolphins—Blowholes—Babies.
  ISBN 0-516-24302-0 (lib. bdg.)—ISBN 0-516-27882-7 (pbk.)
  1. Bottlenose dolphin—Juvenile literature. [1. Bottlenose dolphin. 2. Dolphins.] I. Title. II. Series.

QL737.C432 E26 2003
599.53'3—dc21

                                                    2002156200

Contents

Bottlenose dolphins live in the ocean.

5

Bottlenose dolphins have **fins**.

These fins help dolphins swim.

They can swim very fast.

Bottlenose dolphins have **blowholes** on their heads.

They breathe air through their blowholes.

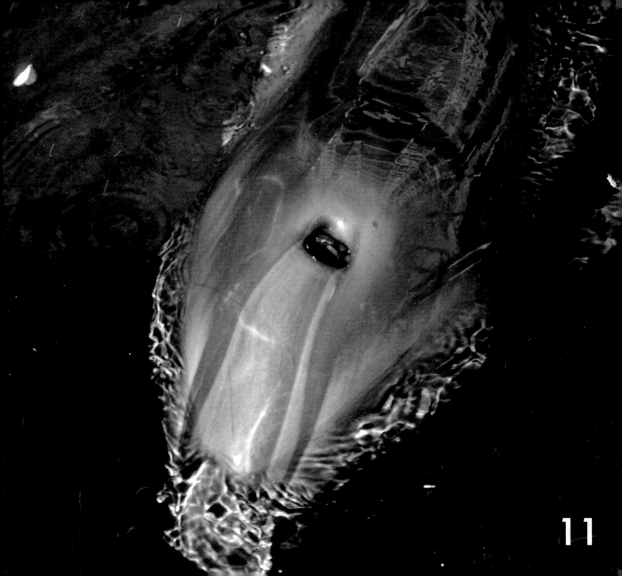

Bottlenose dolphins swim in groups.

A group of bottlenose dolphins is called a **pod**.

Baby bottlenose dolphins are called **calves**.

15

Bottlenose dolphins eat other sea animals.

17

Bottlenose dolphins like to play.

They like to swim near boats.

They can even learn to
do tricks.

Bottlenose dolphins are very
smart animals.

New Words

blowholes (**bloh**-hohlz) openings on dolphins and
whales that are used for breathing

bottlenose dolphins (**baht**-l-nohz **dahl**-finz) small
whales with a round, bottle-shaped nose

calves (**kafz**) young dolphins

fins (**finz**) parts on the body of fish, and other
sea animals, shaped like a flap and used for
moving through water

pod (**pahd**) a group of dolphins

To Find Out More

Books
Dolphins
by Claire Robinson
Heinemann Library

Is a Dolphin a Fish?: Questions and Answers About Dolphins
by Melvin Berger and Gilda Berger
Scholastic

Web Site
Bottlenose Dolphin: ZoomWhales.com
http://www.enchantedlearning.com/subjects/whales/species/
    Bottledolphin.shtml
Learn about bottlenose dolphins, go on a word hunt, and take
the bottlenose dolphin quiz on this Web site.

Index

About the Author

Edana Eckart has written several children's books. She enjoys bike riding with her family.

Reading Consultants

Kris Flynn, Coordinator, Small School District Literacy, The San Diego County Office of Education

Shelly Forys, Certified Reading Recovery Specialist, W.J. Zahnow Elementary School, Waterloo, IL

Sue McAdams, Former President of the North Texas Reading Council of the IRA, and Early Literacy Consultant, Dallas, TX